GLENCOE
LITERATURE

The Reader's Choice

Trinity College
CURRICULUM CENTER

Research and Report
Writing Guide

High School

**Glencoe
McGraw-Hill**

New York, New York   Columbus, Ohio   Woodland Hills, California   Peoria, Illinois

Glencoe/McGraw-Hill

A Division of The **McGraw·Hill** *Companies*

Send all inquiries to:
Glencoe/McGraw-Hill
936 Eastwind Drive
Westerville, Ohio 43081

ISBN 0-02-817565-4

Printed in the United States of America

1 2 3 4 5 6 7 8 9 10 045 03 02 01 00 99

Table of Contents

Introduction

The blackline masters in this booklet provide specific helps to guide the students in all the aspects of research and report writing. They span the gamut of skills from choosing a topic to preparing source cards and from outlining to formulating a list of works cited. The style of documentation presented is strictly based on the guidelines of the Modern Language Association (MLA), a widely accepted standard.

Research and Report Writing
Activity

Choosing a Topic for Research

When you write a research paper, your teacher may have you choose what to write about or may assign a general topic. In either case, you will probably have to focus your topic, that is, narrow it down in order to explore a specific idea. Try to find a topic that interests you as well as one that is appropriate for the assigned length of the paper.

As you narrow your topic, consider who your audience will be. You must provide enough information so that your readers will understand your topic. You do not, however, want to simply tell them what they already know.

Now consider the purpose of your report. What do you want to learn more about and then share with your audience? One good way to start is to ask yourself some questions about your topic. Of course, before you can ask questions, you must know at least a little about the general topic. Find a magazine or encyclopedia article about the topic and do a little preliminary reading.

For example, a student whose general topic was the American Revolution read an encyclopedia article about the Revolution and formulated the following questions:

Why were the British and Americans in conflict?
What were the important events of the American Revolution?
Who were the leaders and important figures in the war?
How did the British and the colonists feel about the war?

After some thinking about these questions, the student decided the following:

I want to write about the leaders of the American Revolution and the events they were involved in.

Further examination of the statement above led the student to more thinking, focusing, and narrowing.

I want to write about Thomas Jefferson's and Benjamin Franklin's roles in the American Revolution, particularly in the writing of the Declaration of Independence.

At this point, the student has a manageable topic. She also has read and thought enough about it to formulate a working idea of what she wants to say about that topic.

Thomas Jefferson and Benjamin Franklin figured prominently in the American Revolution from the Declaration of Independence to the end of the fighting and beyond.

This statement can now serve as a working central idea, the statement that guides future research and gives it direction. The central idea may change as research progresses. As the student locates information, she may find it necessary to further narrow or modify the topic; if so, she will restate her central idea as well.

ACTIVITY
You have been assigned a four-page report on slavery in the United States. Narrow this topic, using the method described on this sheet. Write down your working central idea.

Research and Report Writing
Activity

Setting a Schedule

If you have a project due on a particular date, creating a schedule will help you make sure you get it done on time. An effective schedule includes a starting point, an ending point, and a number of checkpoints in between. The checkpoints consist of separate tasks that must be accomplished as scheduled if the whole project is to move smoothly to its conclusion.

Here are some questions to ask yourself as you create a schedule for your next research paper or other research project:

- What are all the steps in the process?
- When is the work due?
- Are there any special circumstances that I must consider when I create my schedule (such as scheduling interviews, legal holidays when libraries and businesses will be closed, and family events that will require additional time away from my project)?
- Have I allowed a reasonable amount of time for each task?

Here is an example of a schedule one student created for a research report assigned on May 7 and due on May 21.

What to Do	When to Do It	Completed
Prewrite—view larger topic, do preliminary reading, think about audience and purpose, narrow topic, arrive at central idea	5/7–5/8	5/8
Research—find sources, gather information, take notes	5/9–5/14	5/13
Write draft—organize notes, outline, write rough draft	5/15–5/18	5/18
Revise draft—edit, proofread, write final draft	5/19–5/20	5/20
Turn in final report	5/21	5/21

You may have to adjust your scheduled checkpoints if you complete some tasks more quickly than you anticipated or if some tasks take you longer than you anticipated. As you work on your report, continue to use your schedule to check your progress to ensure that you are meeting all your tasks by the final deadline.

ACTIVITY
You have two papers due at midterm—in four weeks. The history paper is supposed to be six pages long; the science paper has to be three pages. Create a schedule to help you get both papers done in four weeks' time. You may use a table, like the one on this sheet, or any other format that helps you record and plan what must be done.

Research and Report Writing
Activity

Finding Information and Evaluating It

After you have chosen your topic and created a schedule, you can begin your research. All the sources you locate will fall into one of two categories: primary and secondary sources.

Primary sources contain firsthand information. Diaries, letters, documents, works of art, photographs, and personal interviews are all primary sources. Primary sources are invaluable for their immediacy. For example, a diary kept by a soldier in World War II would provide a researcher with an intensely personal and immediate view of that period.

Secondary sources contain information that has been gathered and analyzed. Books, magazine articles, and encyclopedias are all secondary sources. These are important because they often present a more objective view than a primary source. A student researching World War II would also consult sources like encyclopedias for more objective information on this period.

Be prepared to carefully read and evaluate the materials you find. You want information that is reliable, containing facts and figures that can be either proved or disproved.

As you consult sources during research, think about the following facts:

- **Author's background:** Check to see whether the author seems qualified to write about this topic. The author should provide facts; any opinions should be backed up with evidence, facts that can be checked.
- **Author's purpose:** Determine whether the purpose is to inform, to prove a point, or to sell a product. (If the purpose is to sell, the document should be evaluated with this in mind.)
- **Source reliability:** Can any facts and figures provided be checked for accuracy? For a Web site, find out who sponsors it, and check all facts you find against another reliable source. If information seems biased, or slanted to a particular point of view, check it against one or two other sources.
- **Date of publication:** Keep in mind that when something was published might affect the information given. Discoveries are made; things are invented; social values change; political divisions are redrawn. Keep these facts in mind when consulting older sources.

ACTIVITY
On a separate piece of paper, classify each source of information as *reliable, unreliable,* or *not certain without further information.* Be ready to give reasons for your choices.

1. An article written by a veterinarian on proper nutrition for dogs and printed in a pamphlet produced by a dog food manufacturer

2. An explanation of why air bags in motor vehicles are a hazard, written and posted on a Web site maintained by an individual

3. A book about management techniques written by a man who created and headed a large corporation

Research and Report Writing
Activity

Conducting Personal Interviews

Before you conduct a personal interview, you must prepare yourself properly. First, you should do some research on your topic to help you choose an appropriate subject for the interview. Then you should prepare some specific questions to ask the person you intend to interview on that subject.

After you have selected a potential subject, follow these steps:

1. Once you get permission to conduct the interview, schedule an appointment at your subject's convenience. Give the person an idea of how much time you think you need. If you want to record the interview, get permission ahead of time.

2. Leave space between questions so you have room to record answers.

3. Avoid asking questions likely to be answered by a simple yes or no. Instead, ask questions that lead your subject to provide information. For example, don't ask: "Do you like the work you do for international disaster relief?" Instead ask: "What do you like about the work you do for international disaster relief?"

4. For the appointment, dress as if you are attending a job interview. Take your notes or questions, two pens, paper, and a clipboard to the interview. If you are using a tape recorder, check your machine's batteries, and practice using the machine beforehand.

5. As you listen, take notes. Do not try to write down everything the subject says. If you do want to write down a quotation, don't be afraid to ask the subject to repeat something. It is better to ask than to get the words wrong.

6. Be a good listener. Use body language to show you are listening even as you take notes.

7. Follow up on interesting comments the subject makes by asking questions. Do not follow your prepared questions so closely that you fail to pursue something that comes up during the interview. Also, if you do not understand something the subject says, ask for an explanation. You could say something like this: "You mentioned the journalists' code of ethics a minute ago. Can you tell me what that is?"

8. When you finish asking questions, thank the subject for his or her time and assistance.

9. Review your notes as soon after the interview as possible. Then record your impressions and any conclusions you have drawn.

10. Write a brief letter of thanks to the subject. In it, mention one detail from the interview that interested you. This will help the subject feel that you were really listening and that the time he or she spent with you was appreciated.

ACTIVITY
Choose a job or career that you are interested in learning about. Conduct some research on the topic, and select a potential subject. If your first subject is not available, continue choosing other possibilities until you find someone who is. Then follow the ten steps on this sheet for conducting a personal interview. When you have completed the interview, prepare an oral presentation in which you tell what you learned and discuss the interview itself, stressing both what you did well and what you would do differently next time.

Research and Report Writing
Activity

Conducting Library Research

You probably have already used many of the resources available in your school or public library. Nevertheless, each new research project you do gives you another chance to use this invaluable source.

Every library collection is a unique combination of printed, computerized, and audiovisual materials. The list below identifies and describes the basic types of library resources:

- **Books:** Most books are in circulation, which means you can check them out. Use the library card catalog or computer catalog to locate books about your topic. Most libraries use the Dewey decimal classification system, in which nonfiction books are numbered and shelved by subject and fiction books are shelved alphabetically by the author's last name. University libraries often use the Library of Congress classification system, which divides books into twenty-one subcategories. A librarian can answer any questions you have regarding these systems of classification.
- **Reference materials:** Most reference materials are not in circulation; you will have to use them in the reference department at the library. The most common reference materials are dictionaries, encyclopedias, atlases, and almanacs.
- **Indexes:** Indexes, such as the *Readers' Guide to Periodical Literature* and *The New York Times Index,* are also located in the reference section for use there. Use these to find magazine or newspaper articles on a particular topic.
- **Periodicals:** Your library receives dozens of magazines and newspapers each week. You can find these in the periodicals department. Current issues of periodicals are usually kept on the shelves. Older issues may be stored on microfilm in the reference department. Some periodical publishers also publish an index of the articles appearing in previous issues. Ask the librarian how to locate these.
- **Audiovisual materials:** Most libraries have an audiovisual department, where audiocassettes, videotapes, and CD-ROMs are shelved. These items are cataloged just as the library's books are, so you can learn what is available by using the card or computer catalog.
- **Computer resources:** Many libraries have computers available to library patrons who want to use the Internet. Other on-line databases or reference materials may also be available. Ask a librarian for help with these.
- **Special collections:** Special collections might include works on state or local history, works of art, government and historical documents, and so on. These items usually do not circulate, but they are available for you to use.

ACTIVITY
Imagine that you have been assigned a research paper on some aspect of your state's history. Go to your school or public library, and locate one source from each of the seven types of library resources listed on this sheet. Make a simple two-column chart in which you record the type of resource and the publication information for it.

Research and Report Writing
Activity

Using the *Readers' Guide to Periodical Literature*

If the research you require must be current, the best place to look may be in a periodical. Magazines that are published weekly or monthly contain up-to-date information. How do you go about finding out which magazine has the information you need? The *Readers' Guide to Periodical Literature* is the key to most magazines that are published in the United States. The *Readers' Guide* is an index that lists all the articles published in hundreds of magazines. Each month your library receives an update to the *Readers' Guide.*

Many libraries now also have a CD-ROM version of the *Readers' Guide.* This allows researchers to search even more thoroughly and quickly on a computer. The advantage of the computerized version is that you can search ten years' worth of magazines at once. When you use the print version, you can only search one month's or, at most, one year's worth of articles at a time.

Information in the *Readers' Guide* is organized by subject or author's last name. Here is an example of a subject entry. The different pieces of information in the entry are identified for you.

subject heading

other subject headings to look under

GREENHOUSE EFFECT

see also

article title

authors of article

"il" means the article is illustrated

Framework Convention on Climate Change
Global Change Research Program (U.S.)
Hot year, but cool response in Congress. G. Vogel and A. Lawler. il
Science v280 no5370 p1684 12 Je '98

title of magazine in which article appears

volume and issue numbers of magazine

page on which article appears

date of magazine: June 12, 1998

The *Readers' Guide* provides further help by including "See also" references. For example, the subject entry for *Great Britain* lists several other subject entries—for example, *England* and *Ireland*—that also include information that may be helpful. Furthermore, broad topics are divided into subtopics. For example, the entry for *Japan* includes the subtopics *commerce, defenses, economic conditions*, and *foreign relations.*

ACTIVITY
Read the subject entry from the *Readers' Guide*. Answer the questions about it that follow.

BALTIMORE ORIOLES (BASEBALL TEAM)
Every fan's fantasy: three Baltimore Orioles die-hards get a chance to tell the team's owner how they really feel.
B. Olney. il *The New York Times Magazine* p94–5 O 18 '98

1. What is the subject heading for this entry? _____

2. Is the article illustrated? _____ How can you tell? _____

3. Who is the author of this article? _____

4. On what date did this article appear? _____

5. On what page or pages is the article printed? _____

Research and Report Writing
Activity

Using Computer Catalogs and Indexes in the Library

A typical library stores its catalog of holdings in a computer. The computer catalog is a very large database that functions as an index, just like the index at the back of a book. You can use the computer catalog to search for resources.

An introductory screen directs you to choose how you want to search. Then you type in what you are searching for by using the author's last name, the title, or the subject. Some computer catalogs allow you to save time by specifying which type of resource you are looking for. For example, you may limit your search to books only or CD-ROMs only.

Some computer catalogs allow you to limit subject searches by using Boolean operators: AND, NOT, and OR. For example, you could perform the following subject search to find out about outer space without having to sort through the many books about space travel.

subject search: outer AND space NOT travel

After you request a search, the computer catalog will perform it and display a list of the results. From that list, you can choose the titles that look most helpful and request additional information on them. Most catalogs even tell you whether the item is available.

If the computer screen displays a message such as "No entries match your search," you should make sure that your subject or keyword was broad enough and that you typed the words correctly. You might want to try a second search with a slightly different word or phrase. It is possible, however, that the library has no resources on that subject or by that author.

Subject indexes, located in the reference department, can lead you to periodical articles or other published forms of information. Because a subject index concentrates on just one subject, it may contain even more thorough coverage than the *Readers' Guide to Periodical Literature.* Some useful subject indexes your library is likely to have include the Art Index, the Biography Index, and the General Sciences Index. Some publications also provide indexes for their own periodicals. The *National Geographic Magazine Cumulative Index* and *The New York Times Index* are two of these.

ACTIVITY

Perform the following searches on the computer catalog at your school or public library. For each search, record the following on a separate sheet of paper: the specific command you typed; the number of entries that matched your search; and the specific title, publication information, and call number of one entry.

1. Search for books by Mark Twain.
2. Search for *Bartlett's Familiar Quotations.*
3. Search for materials about the Appalachian Mountains.

Research and Report Writing
Activity

Searching on the Internet

Through the Internet, a vast electronic communications network that connects computer networks worldwide, you can obtain information from such diverse sources as journals, library catalogs, and other reference sources. The Internet is so vast that to get information quickly, you should use the tools described below:

- **Search engines** are programs that search any type of database for the keywords, or simplified search terms, you type in.
- **Subject directories** are special types of search engines that present a list of topics to help you narrow your search. Every choice you make from the list narrows your topic. At the end of your search, you will have a list of Web sites with information on your specific topic.
- **Metasearch engines** are advanced tools that search several engines at once.

Each search engine or subject directory searches only a small part of the Web. For that reason, it is best to use at least two different search engines or subject directories for a search.

The keywords you use must be exact and specific. For example, a student who wanted to learn about the history of baseball bats might type this.

Typing words such as *baseball, bats, history, legends, manufacture* limits your search.

baseball AND bats AND history AND legends NOT manufacture

Using Boolean operators, such as AND, NOT, and OR, limits your search.

Here are some more tips to help you perform efficient searches on the Internet:

- Most search engines offer advice about themselves. Find a "Tips" button to click on and read what is there.
- Some search engines offer a "More like this" feature. If one Web site listed seems close to what you need, click on "More like this." The search engine will search for similar sites.
- Even if a Web site is disappointing, look for other links that appear in it. A Web site that is unreliable or not helpful might link you to a more reliable and useful site.

ACTIVITY

Imagine that you want to learn about Thomas Jefferson's Statute of Religious Freedom. Conduct a keyword search on the Internet, using a search engine. Use Boolean operators in your search. Then answer the following questions on a separate sheet of paper:

1. What keyword search did you type?

2. How many sites matched your search? Look at the names of the first ten sites.

3. How many of them seem to provide the kind of information you were looking for?

4. If you were to conduct the search again, would you change the keyword search to make it more specific? Explain your answer.

Research and Report Writing
Activity

Evaluating Internet Sources

When you use the Internet for research, you are responsible for evaluating the accuracy and the credibility of the information you find. When the search engine or subject directory displays the results of your search, you have to sort through the sites, using the site names and addresses and any other information provided, to determine which sites best address your topic.

To help you determine whether the site will be useful to you as a research source, ask yourself the following questions: Is it an extensive site with a great deal of information? Is it a two-page site with a brief overview of the topic? Do the site's links look relevant and interesting?

After you determine that a site is a potential source for research, you must begin to critically evaluate its accuracy. You can check a Web site's accuracy by asking and answering the following questions. Keep in mind, however, that to answer these questions you must do research of your own.

- What type of site is it? An informational or news site will probably be more accurate than advocacy or personal pages, which represent single, subjective viewpoints.
- Is the text written so that you can easily understand it?
- Is the text free of grammar and spelling errors?
- Are opinions backed with facts or evidence?
- Are the facts documented? Does the site include a bibliography?
- Is the site reasonably current?
- Are the links within the site appropriate? Do they function?
- Is the site's author clearly identified?
- Is the publisher or sponsor of the site reliable?
- Is the author or publisher accessible by E-mail or postal address?

You should always check another source when you use any Web site for research. If you find information from another source that conflicts with information on the site, check a third source. Do not use information from a site if two other sources conflict with it.

ACTIVITY
Imagine that you are writing a paper for science class about the effectiveness of childhood immunization. Use the Internet to search for a site that appears useful. Evaluate the site's presentation and accuracy. Write down answers to the questions on this sheet to assist you with your evaluation. Record the following information on a separate sheet of paper: your search command, the Web site's name and address, the Web site's author and/or publisher, short answers to the ten evaluation questions listed on this sheet. Then review your answers, and assign an overall score, on a scale of 1 to 5, with 1 being the highest or best. Finally, write a paragraph in which you explain your reasons for assigning that score to the site.

Research and Report Writing
Activity

Using CD-ROMs

If you are doing research that would be aided by looking at pictorial information or listening to a speech, you should consult a CD-ROM (compact disc read-only memory). A CD-ROM is, technically, a media storage device. One CD-ROM can hold as much information as 450 diskettes. Unlike a diskette, however, a CD-ROM can store large amounts of audio, video, and graphic information as well as text. For that reason, programs stored on CD-ROMs are often called multimedia programs.

CD-ROMs can provide diverse information about topics from art to zoology. For example, one particular CD-ROM can even help you find out how to get from your town to the front door of the Empire State Building.

CD-ROMs generally fall into two categories:

- **General reference works:** Many encyclopedias and dictionaries are available on CD-ROM. These resources allow users to carry out keyword searches. Many also include lists of related articles to help users expand or refine their research. The different kinds of information on a CD-ROM can give a more thorough view of a subject than text alone can. There are many possibilities to learn more facets of a subject on a CD-ROM. For example, an article on the space shuttle *Challenger* might include text, pictures of the astronauts, and a video clip of the launch and the explosion that occurred shortly after it. For another project, you could listen to one of President Franklin Roosevelt's fireside chats, originally broadcast over the radio during the 1930s.

- **Special-topic productions:** These CD-ROMs contain current or historical information about a single topic: a person, place, event, period, or culture. Further, more specific topics include scientific information on mammals, weather, or other areas of inquiry. Within a special-topic CD-ROM, users may search for specific pieces of information. In addition, these CD-ROMs usually include photographs, video and sound clips, and still or animated graphics that show how something works or occurs.

ACTIVITY A
Use a multimedia encyclopedia such as *Encarta* or *The World Book Multimedia Encyclopedia* to learn about our solar system. On a separate sheet of paper, record something you learned from the text and from a still or animated illustration. Then describe how these different types of information contributed to your understanding of the solar system.

ACTIVITY B
How do you get from your home to the Empire State Building? Use a CD-ROM such as *TripMaker* to help you plan the trip by automobile. What tools does the program have to help you? Will the program let you customize the trip by taking a detour to Washington, D.C., on the way? Try it and see. Print out the route map that the program develops for you.

Research and Report Writing
Activity

Using Other Electronic Sources

In addition to the Internet and CD-ROMs, other electronic sources can help you expand and refine your research. Do not overlook these sources as you carry out your search for information. You could miss out on some valuable information that might not be found in a book or periodical.

When you do research, investigate the following types of resources:

- **Audiocassettes and compact discs (CDs)** contain audio information. These resources are so common that you may not even think of them as possible sources of information. An audiocassette or a CD may contain music that entertains you or offer information about various styles of music or the work of a composer or a particular group. Audiocassettes and CDs may contain historical broadcasts and programs that were recorded in the days before television and video. These audio sources may also contain the reading of a literary work or actors performing a play.

- **Videocassettes** contain both audio and video information. You might think of videos as purely entertaining; however, many informative educational videos are available. As you would with other resources, you should find out who made a particular video and consider whether there might be any bias that could affect it. Information on videocassette may include a filmmaker's interpretation of a literary work, actual news footage of or about an important twentieth-century event, or a documentary about anything from the Sahara to zebra mussels.

- **Computer diskettes** have largely been replaced by CD-ROMs but are still available. Most programs stored on diskettes, or floppy disks, are written text files; but diskettes may also contain graphics and audio. They are much more limited than CD-ROMs, though, because they have less space for storing information.

- **Digital video discs (DVDs)** are a relatively new technology for storing information. DVDs require a computer with a DVD drive. DVD drives can also play CD-ROMs, but a CD-ROM drive cannot play a DVD. DVDs contain information in a number of formats. They have at least seven times the capacity of a CD-ROM. In fact, an entire feature-length film can be stored on a DVD.

Each of these types of electronic resources has its own advantages. It is up to you, as a researcher, to make use of the different kinds of information these resources contain.

ACTIVITY A
Locate one of each of the following electronic sources at your school or public library. Record the title, disc producer, and call number of each item.

1. Audiocassette
2. Compact
3. Videocassette
4. DVD

ACTIVITY B
On a separate sheet of paper, explain how any of the electronic resources discussed in this worksheet could help you conduct research on each of these topics:

5. *A Tale of Two Cities* by Charles Dickens

6. Firefighting techniques

7. Song lyrics of the 1960s

Research and Report Writing
Activity

Preparing Note Cards

After you have located your sources, you must begin reading thoroughly and taking notes. Remember, the writing you do later will depend on the quality of these notes and the information they contain. Your notes must be organized, thorough, and accurate.

Here are some important points to consider as you take notes:

- Do not take notes on everything you read. You will end up with too many cards, and the information you find will probably repeat itself. You must choose the information that you believe pertains to your report.
- Read carefully and critically. Start with the most comprehensive sources, such as encyclopedia articles. Then move on to more specialized sources. Record only new pieces of information that you encounter.
- Pay attention to context. Taking a piece of information out of context could lead you to provide false information or reach a faulty conclusion in your paper. When taking notes, make sure you record the supporting information an author provides so that you have evidence to back up your statements.

Here is a sample note card.

(A) **Citation**
This one includes the title and author's last name

(B) **Source number**
The bibliography card for Source 3 holds the complete bibliographic citation for this source

(C) **Subject** of card

Justinia's Rise Murphy   3

childhood

"Justinia Clark's . . . running for class president stunned her classmates. They regarded
her as a painfully shy girl . . . afraid of the
sound of her own voice."

Notes

12   page 45

(E) **Card number**

(D) **Page number**
on which information was found

Aside from the notes themselves, notice that the card contains certain information:

(A) **Citation:** This may include just the title, the title and author's last name, or perhaps an article title and the title of the magazine it appeared in.

(B) **Source number:** This is the number of the bibliography card that contains the complete bibliographic citation.

(C) **Subject of card:** Each note card should have one kind of information on it to help you organize your notes. Write the subject of each card just above the notes you record on that card. For example, on the card shown above, the student noted that the subject was childhood. Writing subjects on each card will help you later when you begin to write your paper.

(D) **Page number(s):** Each note card should include the page number(s) for all the information you found.

(E) **Card number:** Many researchers also number their note cards sequentially.

On the card shown above, the student quoted the material directly. Direct quotations, which are taken word for word from the source, should be put in quotation marks. The other two methods of recording notes from a source, paraphrasing and summarizing, do not require quotation marks.

Research and Report Writing
Activity

When you paraphrase a statement, you rewrite it in your own words. You might paraphrase the quotation on the note card above as follows:

Justinia Clark's classmates considered her so shy that she would be afraid of speaking. They were surprised at her announcement that she would run for class president.

When you write a summary, your statement contains only the most important pieces of information without descriptive details. The following note card shows a summary of the original quotation.

> <u>Justinia's Rise</u> Murphy   3
> childhood
> Justinia Clark surprised her classmates by
> announcing that she would run for class president.
> They considered her to be an extremely shy girl
> who seemed to be afraid of speaking.
> 12   page 45

Keep in mind that when you write a note as a direct quotation, you have the option of paraphrasing or summarizing it later. If you take a note in a paraphrased or summarized statement, you cannot turn it into a direct quotation unless you return to the original source and recopy it.

ACTIVITY
Following is another excerpt from the book about Justinia Clark. Create one note card on which you paraphrase the text. Create a second note card on which you summarize the text. Be sure to include all the pieces of information that must be on each note card.

Once Justinia overcame her initial hesitancy, she embarked on a brilliant political career. Her passion for reform and desire to create a more caring society shone through in her campaign speeches. This affected her audiences, and many of the women who had recently been granted the right to vote felt she was the perfect person to represent their interests. Miss Justinia Clark soon became Senator Clark.

—L. Murphy, *Justinia's Rise*, page 62

Research and Report Writing
Activity

Avoiding Plagiarism

Plagiarism, or presenting someone else's words or ideas as if they were your own, is a serious issue. Plagiarism carries severe penalties, ranging from failing a course to being expelled from school. It is always best to err on the side of caution. Cite the source if you have any question about whether or not you are using another writer's words or original ideas. You are plagiarizing if you do any of the following without marking the text as a quotation and giving the author credit:

- repeat a sentence or more of another person's words
- present an original term or phrase as your own
- present another person's argument or line of thinking as your own

As a student researcher, you must take particular care to document everything that you borrow. Even summaries and paraphrases should be attributed. That is why it is so important to take notes carefully so that you know which sentences, phrases, and ideas are yours and which are the author's.

When you are citing another source in a research paper, you may set up the citation in several ways. If you are using a direct quotation, you can cite the source either immediately following the quotation or in a footnote or endnote. The following example is a direct quote from page 712 of *Reading* by L. T. Nelson that a student used on a card: "Reading to your children is important because it fosters a love of books."

Following are some examples of how the student might use the quotation for a research paper. The examples in the left column are plagiarism. The examples in the right column are properly cited.

Plagiarism	Correct Use
Quoted: I believe that reading to [your] children is important because it fosters a love of books.	I agree with Nelson's statement that "reading to your children is important because it fosters a love of books." (712)
Paraphrased: In fact, it is important for parents to read to their children because it fosters a love of books.	In fact, it is important for parents to read to their children because it fosters a love of books (Nelson 712).
Use of idea: Parents ought to read to their children in order to foster a love of books in them.	Parents ought to read to their children in order to foster a love of books in them. (Nelson 712) (For a discussion of the possible ways to cite this as an endnote or footnote, see Sheet 31.)

ACTIVITY
Read the following directly quoted sentences from L. T. Nelson's *Reading*. Then write a paragraph using the information in those sentences. Be sure to cite each piece of information properly.

1. "You should set a time to read with your child every night." (page 78)
2. "You and your child will share magical moments if you read together." (page 92)
3. "Always be sure to keep interesting books for your children around the house." (page 109)

Research and Report Writing
Activity

Developing a Working Bibliography

As you gather sources for your research, keep a working bibliography, a record of every source that you consult. Your working bibliography will change frequently during your research as you add sources, refocus your topic, or change or modify your central idea.

You can create your working bibliography by writing down each source with its bibliographical information on a three-by-five-inch index card. Assign each source a number, and record the number on your bibliography card. This will make it easier to organize your cards later. Also note the call number and the location of the source if you use more than one library. You can also keep your working bibliography on computer files and add, delete, or rearrange them as you make changes.

Several steps are involved in creating a working bibliography:

1. Investigate and compile possible sources.

2. As you take notes, write down the source's title, author, and publication information. The publication information varies, depending on the type of source used. The publication information for a book usually includes the name of the publisher, the city where the publisher is located, and the year of publication. In a book, this information can be found on the title page and the copyright page, which usually follows the title page. The format shown below follows the style guidelines of the Modern Language Association (MLA).

Title Page	On the page after the title page look for a line like this:
Title ——————— Smith's Book	Copyright © 1999 by X. Smith ——— **Year of publication**
Author ——————— X. Smith	
	OR look for a section like this:
	Published by
	Jones and Company, Inc. ——— **Publisher**
Publisher ——— Jones and Company, Inc.	New York, NY ——————— **City of publisher**
City of publisher ——— New York	Copyright 1999 X. Smith ——— **Year of publication**

3. Change your working bibliography as you refine and revise your paper. Make sure you include cards for sources you use. Set aside those cards for sources you do not use.

ACTIVITY

A student writing a paper on folksingers Jere Doe and Sarita Lan and their influence on 1960s society used the books listed below. Then the student decided to focus on Lan. On a separate sheet of paper, list only the books that should be in her new bibliography and explain why they should be.

1. Doe, J. *Folk Life.* New York: Zone Books, 1995.

2. Rone, Ida. *60s Folk Artists.* Chicago: AB Press, 1998.

3. Trent, B. *Sarita's Rise.* Miami: Nod, 1998.

4. Ar, Cyrus. *Doe, Lan, Smid, and Teag: Four Legends.* Memphis: Moose Press, 1997.

5. Doe-Irving, Miranda. *Life with Doe.* New York: Corey Press, 1999.

Research and Report Writing
Activity

Creating Bibliography Cards for Books

It is important to keep track of every source that you consult by making a bibliography card for it. Each bibliography card in your working bibliography must contain complete publication information. Also, remember to assign a source number and to note the library call number of a source on its bibliography card.

Following are two bibliography cards for books. The first example shows how to organize and punctuate the publication information. Notice how the punctuation helps keep the pieces of information separate and distinct. The second example shows an actual bibliography card. Remember that you should have five pieces of information on a bibliography card for a book.

Source no.

Author's last name, Author's first name.
   Title of book. City in which book was
   published: Publisher's name, date of
   publication.
Location   Call no.

5

Shoumatoff, Alex. Legends of the American
   Desert. New York: Alfred A. Knopf, 1997.

Clarkstown Public Library   746.92 Sh

ACTIVITY

Each of the following numbered items contains the publication information for a book and other relevant information for a bibliography card. On a separate sheet of paper, create a correctly organized and punctuated bibliography card for each book.

1. Source 1, *Architects of the American Century* by David F. Schmitz, Imprint Publications, 1999, Chicago, Morris County Public Library, Call No. 765.82 Sch

2. Source 2, David Heath, *Congress of the United States* 1999: Mankato, MN: Capstone Press, Morris High School, Call No. 760.32 Hea

Research and Report Writing
Activity

Creating Bibliography Cards for Periodicals

With periodicals, as with all other sources, create a bibliography card even before you start taking notes. Bibliography cards for periodicals require the information shown in the example to the right. You also might want to note the location and type of source material (microfilm, bound copy) so that you know where the source is located.

Source no.

Author's last name, Author's first name.
"Title of article." Title of magazine
Day Month Year of magazine issue: first
and last page numbers.

Location

The example to the right shows an actual bibliography card. Notice that when a magazine article has more than one author, only the first author's name is reversed. Since this particular article is many pages long but the pages are not consecutive, the student cites just the first page, then adds a plus sign to show that the article continues.

4

Pringle, Heather Anne, and Robert Stewart.
"Traces of Ancient Mariners Found in
Peru." Science 18 Sept. 1998: 1775+.

Westwood Public Library
Bound magazines

The format for documenting newspaper articles is slightly different from that of magazine articles. The sample newspaper article to the right has no byline, or author credit. If an author is named, that information goes first in the bibliographic entry. Note how the name of the newspaper appears: The name of the city is not part of the newspaper's title, so the city name goes in brackets following the title. Notice, too, that when citing the page number, the student also includes the section number or letter (most newspapers are divided into sections, each with a number—1, 2, 3, and so on—or a letter—A, B, C, and so on.) In the sample that follows, the section is A.

6

"Lost Empires in the Americas." Globe and Mail
[Toronto] 2 Apr. 1996: A1+.

High school library
Microfilm

ACTIVITY
Rewrite the following periodical references according to the format shown on this sheet:

1. Russo R. M., and Paul G. Silver The Andes' Deep Origins Natural History Feb 1995 52–92.
2. Moffat Anne Simon Biogeographers Take a New View of the Ancient Andes Science 7 June 1996 1420–21

Research and Report Writing
Activity

Creating Bibliography Cards for Videocassettes, Films, and Audiocassettes

Videocassettes, films, and audiocassettes require slightly different information in their bibliographic entries. The following examples show how to format and punctuate information on bibliography cards for videocassettes and films. The only difference in their formats is the notation "Videocassette" in the citation on the left. If you cannot find all the information, provide as much as you can.

```
                                    7 [Source no.]
The Video Anthology and Music of the Americas.
   [Title.] Dir. Mark Orion. [Director.] Perf. Gayle
   Matthias. [Performer.] Videocassette. [Video-
   cassette.] Multicultural Media, [Dist.] 1995.
   [year released.]
Public library
AV Vid [location]
```

```
                                    8 [Source no.]
Catch the Sun. [Title of film.] Dir. Marco Lopez.
   [Director's name.] Perf. Danielle Arzolla.
   [Performers' names—optional.] United Films,
   [Distributor] 1999. [year of release.]
```

The format for bibliographic entries for audiocassettes varies. In general, whatever you want to emphasize goes first in your entry, as shown in the examples below, which list the composer or the performer first. The student uses the notation "n.d." which stands for "no date," because the release date was not provided. Spoken word recordings such as books on cassette should contain the same information as the example but list the author first.

```
                                    10 [Source no.]
Francesco Geraldo. [Name of composer.]
   Music of the Incas. [Title of recording.]
   Perf. Ayllu Sulca. [Performers' names.] Audio-
   cassette. [Audiocassette.] Lyrichord Disc,
   [Manufacturer,] n.d. [year of release.]
Duncan Public Library [location]
AV Mus
```

```
                                    11 [Source no.]
Dominic Cultano. [Name of performer.]
   "Like the Morning." [Title of song—optional.]
   Songs for Seasons. [Title of recording.]
   Audiocassette. [Audiocassette.] Arista,
   [Distributor,] 2000. [year of release.]
```

ACTIVITY

The following illustration shows a computer catalog entry for an audiocassette. On this catalog screen, the "author" refers to the performer. Sort out the information you need, and create a bibliography card.

TITLE:	Kingdom of the Sun: Peru's Inca Heritage
AUTHOR:	Lewiston, David
CALL NUMBER:	AV Kin
PUBLISHED:	New York, NY: Elektra/Nonesuch, 1998
MEDIA:	audiocassette–1 sound cassette
SUBJECT:	folk music–Peru

Research and Report Writing
Activity

Creating Bibliography Cards for CD-ROMs

This bibliography card shows how to organize and punctuate the necessary publication information for a CD-ROM:

> Source no.
>
> Author's last name, Author's first name.
>   Title of publication. Name of editor, compiler, or
>   translator, if given. CD-ROM. Edition, release,
>   or version number, if appropriate. Place of pub-
>   lication: Name of publisher, year of publication.
> Location   Call no.

Not all of this information will be available on every CD-ROM. Multimedia encyclopedias, for example, usually do not have authors listed. In that case, begin the entry with the title of the CD-ROM. As a general rule, include as much information on your bibliography card as you can find. Here is an example of a bibliography card for a CD-ROM:

> 3
>
> Let's Visit South America. CD-ROM.
>   Fairfield, CT: Queue, 1998.
>
> High school library   980 L649

ACTIVITY A
Use the information shown on this CD-ROM to create a bibliography card.

BATLAS ARTS®
3D ATLAS
Version 2.1

MACINTOSH CD-ROM

©1997 BATLAS ARTS

ACTIVITY B
Use the computer catalog at your school or public library to locate a CD-ROM to use in conducting research on Christopher Columbus. Create a bibliography card for the source you find.

Research and Report Writing
Activity

Creating Bibliography Cards for Other Electronic Sources

If you use information stored on a diskette or from another electronic source in your research, use the card on the right as a guide in creating a bibliography card for it:

> Source no.
>
> Author's last name, Author's first name.
>   Title of publication. Name of editor, compiler, or
>   translator, if given. Diskette. Edition, release, or
>   version number, if appropriate. Place of pub-
>   lication: Name of publisher, date of publication.
> Location

Because compact discs are so common, you do not have to note "compact disc" in the bibliographic entry. Entries for CDs can vary in which information comes first, depending on whether the researcher wants to emphasize the composer, the performer, or the title of the work. If you use audio information stored on a compact disc, your bibliography card should look like the card on the right.

> Source no.
>
> Title. Director's name. Performers' names
>   [optional]. Distributor, year of release.
>
>
> Location

Here is a sample bibliography card for a CD. The student has chosen to list the title of the work first. The director, the performing group, and the compiler are also listed to further identify the recording.

> 12
>
> Music of the Andes. Dir. Victor Jara. Perf.
>   Inti-Illimani. Hemisphere, 1998.
>
>
> City Public Library

ACTIVITY
The following bibliography card entries are incorrect. Rewrite the entries correctly on a separate piece of paper.

D K Multimedia, 1998, *Eyewitness Children's Encyclopedia,* diskette Smithsonian/Folkways, prod. Rounder Records, dist. "Mountain Music of Peru." compact disc. 1994

Research and Report Writing
Activity

Creating Bibliography Cards for On-line Sources

To create a bibliography card for an on-line source, scroll to the bottom of the first page of the Web site. Most Web pages provide some information about who wrote or copyrighted the material, who maintains the site, and when the site was last updated. In some cases, you may have to click on a link labeled "About the site" or "Info" to reveal that information. When you use information from an on-line source in your research paper, use the bibliography card on the right as a guide.

Here is a sample bibliography card for an on-line source: Notice that the first item listed is the title of the document.

If the on-line source you are using includes material that has been published both electronically and in print, you must add a few more pieces of information. For example, if you refer to an on-line version of the book *Great Expectations,* your citation must include publication information for both the electronic and print versions. You should note the title of the book, placing this after the title of the document or posting. Then note the edition, city, publisher, and date the book was published, placing this after the editor, compiler, or translator of the on-line source. On the right is a sample bibliography card for an on-line source containing copyrighted print and electronic material.

Source no.

Author's last name, first name. "Title of article."
Title of document. Name of editor. Version number.
Date of electronic publication or last update.
Name of institution sponsoring Web site. Date
you used source [without a period] <Electronic
address of source>

12

SALSA: Scientific Alliance for South America.
Klaus Battaille, dir. Feb. 1999. Mar. 17, 1999
<http://www.dgf.uchile.cl/salsa.html>

14

Twain, Mark. "The INTERNET WIRETAP First Elec-
tronic Edition of The Adventures of Tom Sawyer."
The Adventures of Tom Sawyer, 2d edition.
New York: Dutton, 1997. June 1993. May 19, 1999
<http://www.cs.cmu.edu/People/rgs/sawyr-ftitle.html>

ACTIVITY

Create a bibliography card for the following on-line source. On March 3 1999, a student visited the Andean Botanical Information System Web site at <www.sacha.org>. The information was from a portion of the site titled "Environments," and had been updated the day before. The site is sponsored and maintained by The Field Museum of Chicago, IL. All material in the site is copyrighted by Michael Dillon and Nancy Hensold.

Research and Report Writing
Activity

Organizing Note Cards

There are several possible approaches or ways of organizing and presenting information when you write a research report. The one you choose depends on your topic and your central idea. The chart below shows four common approaches and topics that lend themselves to a particular approach.

Approaches	Topics
Chronological, placing events in a particular order	Battles of World War II, the life story of Benjamin Franklin, a step-by-step explanation of how to plant a vegetable garden
Cause and effect	The causes of the Revolutionary War, the effects of growing plants under full-spectrum light bulbs, the events leading to the breakup of the Soviet Union
Order of importance	The results of a survey on teen curfews, the results of an experiment in which you evaluate how long it takes various packaging substances to degrade
Compare and contrast	The similarities and differences between early Native American groups, evaluating a presidential race by comparing and contrasting the candidates, comparing and contrasting the American home front with the British home front during World War I

After you determine the approach you want to use to organize your paper, you must organize your note cards accordingly. When you took notes, you wrote one idea, or one piece of information, about a single subtopic on each note card. Now you can divide your note cards into separate piles by subtopic. For example, if you are comparing the American and British home fronts, your first step is to separate the cards about the American home front from the cards about the British. Then you can separate each stack into sub-subtopics, such as shortages, raising money, women and work, and so on. If your notes are on computer, you can create different files for the subtopics and then work from there.

ACTIVITY A
Suppose you are writing a paper on the steps required to apply for a part-time job. What approach will be best for this paper? Explain your response on a separate sheet of paper.

ACTIVITY B
Imagine that you are researching the birth and growth of the personal computer industry and the resulting changes in American society. What approach will be best for this paper? Into what two categories should you separate your note cards? What subtopics might there be within those categories? List at least three. Write your answers on a separate sheet of paper.

Research and Report Writing
Activity

Developing an Outline

An outline is a summary of the main points about your topic and the ideas that support them. While you were taking notes from sources, you began to group the note cards into different classifications. As you decided how to classify and organize your notes, you took the first step in making a working outline. At this point, you jot down your first informal outline.

As you conduct further research, you also continue to write and revise your outline. The following steps will help you make a working outline that will eventually become the formal outline you will use to prepare the first draft of your paper:

1. Group together note cards on similar topics. Use each group as a main topic in your outline.

2. Within each group, place similar note cards together, forming subgroups. Use each subgroup as a subheading in your outline.

3. To keep yourself focused, write your central idea at the top of your outline.

4. Arrange main topics to build on your central idea.

5. Under each main topic, arrange subheadings so that they build on the main topic in a logical way.

6. Copy all points in outline form on a sheet of paper, creating a working draft of your outline.

7. Revise and rewrite your outline as you continue your research.

8. Keep all note cards, even those that do not fit under any heading. You may need them later.

9. Prepare a formal outline when you complete your research and your working outline.

Here is an example of a section of a working outline with a central idea, three main topics, and subheadings.

Central idea: I will compare and contrast eight different types of conservation.

    I. Soil conservation
       A. Description
       B. Problems
       C. Solutions
    II. Water conservation
       A. Description
       B. Problems
       C. Solutions
   III. Forest conservation
       A. Description
       B. Problems
       C. Solutions

ACTIVITY
Write an outline for a paper on how to qualify for a driver's license in your state. Think of the topic in terms of the process of acquiring skills, meeting requirements, taking tests, and so on. In your outline, include three main topics, with at least two subtopics for each.

Research and Report Writing
Activity

Developing a Thesis Statement

When you chose a topic to research, you also developed a central idea to guide that research. Now is the time to polish the central idea you are working with to use as your thesis statement. A thesis statement is a concise statement of what you will prove, expand on, or illustrate in your paper. Here are four major types of thesis statements and examples of each.

Type of Thesis Statement	Description	Example
Original	Demonstration of new information you have developed	Survey of students and teachers on ways they conserve resources by reducing, reusing, and recycling
Evaluative	Statement of your opinion on a topic	Discussion of why you do or do not support affirmative action programs in colleges
Summary	Report consisting primarily of the ideas of others	Archaeological findings–past and present–uncovered at Pompeii and what they indicate about the city's culture
Combination	Combines any two or all three of the types above	Summary about the Lincoln-Douglas debates and your opinion of the candidates' ability to persuade

After you have determined which type of thesis statement best lends itself to your topic, you can ask yourself the following questions to guide you in writing it:

1. What was my original central idea?

2. How has it changed as I have conducted my research?

3. What is the concise question I am trying to answer in my paper?

Writing down the answers to these questions will help you structure your thesis statement. Here is how one student answered the questions. Notice how her answers led to her thesis statement.

Original central idea: *Describe the various types of conservation.*
Changes: *Conservation is too broad. Narrow it down to describing a few types.*
Question: *What are the problems and solutions involved in water conservation and forest conservation?*
Thesis statement: *Conservation of water and forest resources present several serious problems, but solutions to these problems can be found.*

ACTIVITY
Read the following thesis statements. Choose the best one and explain your choice.

1. An independent consulting firm reports that a modern, high-speed transit system is just what our city's commuters need for safe, efficient travel.

2. The reintroduction of wolves into Yellowstone National Park, though controversial, has been a successful process for the wolves, for the park itself, and for park visitors.

3. The works of Flemish painter Pieter Brueghel the Elder are vibrant.

Research and Report Writing
Activity

Writing a Research Paper That Explains a Process

When you explain a process in a research paper, you are using a chronological approach. Your goal is to place a series of steps or events in the order necessary to achieve the desired results. For example, you would use this approach to explain how a bill becomes a law or what you need to do to conduct a scientific experiment. Additional examples of topics that lend themselves to a chronological approach include biographies and historical topics.

The general approach for this type of paper is to break the process into steps and to explain each step in the order in which it happens. Use transitions to keep the order of steps or events clear. The words *first, then, now, next, meanwhile, later,* and *afterward* are among many that indicate at which stage of the process something happens.

Here is a brief example of a set of steps or events that will become part of the outline for a process paper:

1. A revenue bill is introduced in the U.S. House of representatives.

2. The Speaker of the House assigns the bill to a committee for study.

3. The committee studies the bill and hears testimony from experts.

4. The bill goes on a calendar, a list of bills awaiting action.

5. Consideration by the House begins with a second reading of the bill.

6. If the bill passes, it goes to the Senate.

ACTIVITY
The following events or steps are from a research paper that explains the major territorial acquisitions of the United States from 1776 to 1898. The steps have been scrambled. Read and reorganize them in chronological order.

1. The federal government paid France $15 million for the Louisiana Purchase of 1803.

2. The Oregon country cession extended the western border of the United States to the Pacific Ocean in 1846.

3. The Hawaii annexation of 1898 gave the United States its largest present overseas possession.

4. The Florida cession of 1819 gave the United States the areas then called East Florida and West Florida.

5. The thirteen colonies occupied what became the original area of the United States.

6. The Texas annexation of 1845 added what was then the nation's largest state.

7. The addition of 1783 more than doubled the territory of the United States.

8. The federal government paid Russia $7.2 million for the Alaska Purchase of 1867.

9. The United States paid Mexico $10 million for the Gadsden Purchase of 1853.

10. The federal government paid Mexico $15 million for the land that was part of the Mexico cession of 1848.

11. The Red River cession was included in a treaty between the United States and Great Britain in 1818.

Research and Report Writing
Activity

Writing a Research Paper That Compares and Contrasts

When you write a compare-and-contrast paper, you explain how events, people, places, or ideas are alike and different. Then, you draw a conclusion based on these comparisons and contrasts.

The first step in writing a compare-and-contrast paper is choosing subjects that are well balanced in terms of similarities and differences. The next step is to analyze the subjects, perhaps by using a Venn diagram. Here is an example of a Venn diagram used in this way.

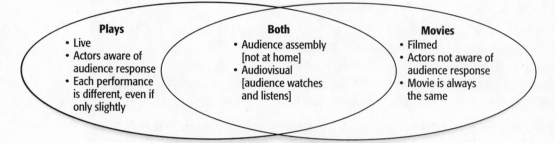

Plays
- Live
- Actors aware of audience response
- Each performance is different, even if only slightly

Both
- Audience assembly [not at home]
- Audiovisual [audience watches and listens]

Movies
- Filmed
- Actors not aware of audience response
- Movie is always the same

After you have written a thesis statement in which you identify the subjects and the central idea of your paper, you can organize your compare-and-contrast paper in one of two ways. The first method is the block method, sometimes called the whole-to-whole method.

The other method of organization is the feature-by-feature, or part-to-part, method. See the examples below.

Block Method
Subject 1: college basketball
    Feature 1: length of game
    Feature 2: three-point line
    Feature 3: defense rules
Subject 2: professional basketball
    Feature 1: length of game
    Feature 2: three-point line
    Feature 3: defense rules

Feature-by-Feature Method
Feature 1: length of game
    Subject 1: college basketball
    Subject 2: professional basketball
Feature 2: three-point line
    Subject 1: college basketball
    Subject 2: professional basketball
Feature 3: defense rules
    Subject 1: college basketball
    Subject 2: professional basketball

ACTIVITY A
Plan a research paper in which you are to compare and contrast two countries. Country A is a rich, coastal, industrial country that contains rain forests. Country B is a poor, coastal, agricultural country that contains deserts. Both are popular with tourists. On a separate sheet of paper, make a Venn diagram to determine the countries' distinguishing and similar characteristics.

ACTIVITY B
Using the subjects from Activity A, create an outline for a compare-and-contrast paper. Use either the block method or the feature-by-feature method.

Research and Report Writing
Activity

Writing a Research Paper That Explains Cause and Effect

In a cause-and-effect paper, you answer one or both of these questions: Why did something happen? What were the effects of this event? You must also provide evidence to show that the causes and effects presented are valid ones. The type of evidence depends on the subject of the paper. For example, in a scientific research paper, you should provide scientific data to support statements. For historic causes and effects, you might look at contemporary accounts, that is, accounts from the time the events occurred, for supporting material.

There are three ways to organize a cause-and-effect paper:

- Focus on the causes of an event by devoting most of the body of the paper to a discussion of how and why particular events cause or caused another event to happen.
- Focus on the causes of an event as well as the effects of that event.
- Focus on a sequence of causes and effects, with each one leading to the next. Keep in mind, however, that a cause may have more than one effect and an effect may have more than one cause.

The sequence of cause and effect can be mapped with a sequence chain. For example, a student doing a paper on a local flood drew the sequence chain shown below to map out her paper.

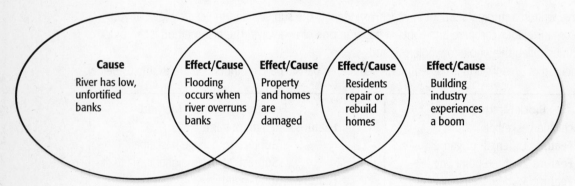

Cause	**Effect/Cause**	**Effect/Cause**	**Effect/Cause**	**Effect/Cause**
River has low, unfortified banks	Flooding occurs when river overruns banks	Property and homes are damaged	Residents repair or rebuild homes	Building industry experiences a boom

When you gather information for a cause-and-effect paper, you must think about obvious as well as hidden causes. You must also decide whether there is a main cause. If there is, you should present it last. The main cause will have more impact if you save it until last and devote more space to it.

When you are focusing on the effects of an event, consider both obvious and subtle effects. Also, remember that although some effects are immediate, others occur over time. Keep in mind, though, that you must include evidence to back up the effects you discuss.

ACTIVITY A
Suppose you want to research the successful campaign tactics of a politician. What method of organization would work best for this topic? Explain why on a separate sheet of paper.

ACTIVITY B
Plan a research paper that examines a sequence of causes and effects. Choose a topic that interests you. Then use a sequence chain like the one shown on this sheet to identify the sequence of events. Construct your chain on a separate sheet of paper.

Research and Report Writing
Activity

Revising an Outline

As you continue research, you may uncover new information, get a new idea, or discover a weakness or omission in your outline. Sometimes ideas that looked good in the early stages of research simply don't work out the way you had hoped, either because you can't locate information or information you find disproves your original ideas. The more research you do, the more likely the need for adjustments. Such adjustments call for revisions in your outline.

Here is an example of a revised outline. At the left is the student's original outline. This outline shows that she had planned to compare and contrast communication in the past with communication in the present. As she worked, though, she discovered she needed more support for the points she made. She also found more information she wanted to work in.

I. In the past
   A. Written correspondence
      1. Formal
      2. Informal
   B. Telephone communication
      1. Formal
      2. Informal
II. In the present
   A. Written correspondence
      1. Frequency
      2. Formality
   B. Telephone communication
      1. Frequency
      2. Formality

I. In the past
   A. Written correspondence
      1. Invitations
      2. Thank-you letters
      3. Business correspondence
      4. Friendly letters
   B. Telephone communication
      1. Busy signals
      2. No answer
      3. Direct conversation, not messages
II. In the present
   A. Written correspondence
      1. Handwritten or typed letters less common
      2. Business correspondence little changed
      3. E-mail more frequent, less formal
   B. Telephone communication
      1. Brief messages
      2. Business previously conducted by mail now done over phone
      3. Little personal contact

Although the student didn't change the main headings and subheadings in her outline, she added many specific details. She did not discard any information, but instead added additional support. She even made note of a special anecdote she wanted to use in a particular spot. Now that her outline is revised, she can reorganize her note cards to reflect the changes.

ACTIVITY
The student who is writing about communications past and present has a problem. She can estimate from the note cards that her paper is going to be far longer than the length specified by the teacher, so she must further narrow her topic. Revise the outline so that it focuses on either the "In the past" portion or the "In the present" portion. Add a total of five more subheads and specific details to the section you have chosen to focus on.

Research and Report Writing
Activity

Formatting a Research Paper

As you prepare to write your rough draft, consider how you must format the final paper. (If you are typing or using a word processing program, you can set margins and set off quotations, for example.) This gives you a good start toward formatting the final draft of your report.

Margins	Leave a one-inch margin at top, bottom, and both sides of every page.
Spacing	Double-space every line of text. Do not leave extra space after your title or between paragraphs.
Identifying information	If your teacher does not require a cover page, in the upper right corner of the first page, put your name, your teacher's name, the class name, and the date, each on a separate line.
	On page 2 and all following pages, put your last name and the page number in the upper right corner, one-half inch from the top.
Title	Center the title of the paper on the double-spaced line below your identifying information.
Paragraphs	Indent the first line of each paragraph five spaces, or one-half inch.
Short quotations	Run short quotations in with the text, but put quotation marks around them.
Long quotations	Set off long quotations (more than four typewritten lines) by indenting them one inch from the left margin. Do not indent from the right margin. Do not use quotation marks.
Works cited list	Following the text of your paper, start a new page with the heading "Works Cited" centered below your identifying information.
	Double-space each entry in your list. For entries that are more than one line long, indent the second and following lines one-half inch from the left margin.

ACTIVITY
Use a typewriter or computer to type the first page of text for a research paper, using the material below. Be sure to follow the guidelines for margins, spacing, identifying information, title, and paragraphs.

Stephanie Haban, Mr. Porter, Life Science, September 16, 2000

The Use of Echolocation in Dolphins and Other Members of the Family *Delphinidae*

Most of us are familiar with the friendly, chattering image of a dolphin in an aquatic exhibition. We know very little, however, about dolphins that live in their natural environment—the ocean. What do they eat? How do they find their food? How do they distinguish between friend and foe? The answer to all these questions, at least in part, is echolocation.

Research and Report Writing
Activity

Writing a Rough Draft

You have gathered all your resource materials, sorted through your notes, composed an outline, made adjustments to it, and considered the formatting of your paper. Now it is time for you to start writing your first version of your paper, your rough draft. When you begin, don't worry about whether the writing is perfect. Just follow your outline and get all your notes and ideas on paper. You can fine-tune later.

Here are some tips to help your rough draft flow smoothly:

- Follow your outline when you write your rough draft. Post the most recent version of your outline where you can see it, and refer to it frequently. Move from topic to subtopic to details one step at a time, constructing your paragraphs so that they follow the model provided by your outline.
- Do not feel that you must start your draft with your introduction. You may be more comfortable writing the body of your paper first. The inspiration for your attention-getting introduction may come as you write the body.
- When you do draft your introduction, think of a way to grab your readers' attention. You may do this by opening with a startling or unusual fact or anecdote, a question, or a quotation. Whatever you use, it should make your reader want to continue beyond the first paragraph. Your introduction should also include your thesis statement. You may have to alter this statement slightly so that it works in your introductory paragraph.
- Do not get stuck on a word. If you cannot think of just the right word, write down the best one you can think of. Then circle it as a reminder to find a more appropriate word later.
- Try to make transitions and logical connections from one idea to the next and between paragraphs. At the same time, recognize that you probably will not get them all the first time. Just move on, and then come back to them later.
- When you include quotations, statistics, or anything that requires documentation, make a note of this in your draft. The easiest way to do this is to write and circle the number of the note card on which you recorded each piece of information. The circled number will alert you to the fact that you must document the information later, when your draft is closer to your final paper. You will do this in one of two ways, as explained on page 33.
- When you write your conclusion, use words or phrases such as *finally, in conclusion,* or *to conclude* to signal the closing of your paper. Your conclusion may also include a summary of your thesis statement or a restatement of the question—and the answer—your paper explores.

ACTIVITY
Write a strategy for dealing with each of the following aspects of a rough draft:

1. Introduction

_____

2. Specific words

_____

3. Transitions

_____

Research and Report Writing
Activity

Using Quotations

Researchers use quotations in their written reports for many reasons. Quotations provide evidence or help support opinions. They add interest or "flavor." They also lend credibility to the researcher's work.

As a researcher and writer, you may quote a word, a phrase, a sentence, or a longer passage of someone else's writing in your report. Of course, you must always give credit to your source, and you must be as clear as possible about your sources. You can work a quotation into your research paper in one of several ways. Study the chart below.

Material Quoted	How to Use the Quotation in Your Paper
Word or phrase	Include the quotation in a sentence of your own. The quotation must fit with the structure and tense of the sentence surrounding it. For her birthday, Aaron presented Lily with a new watch that was **"fancier than anything she had ever imagined,"** with diamonds sparkling across the band (Smythe 28).
Sentence	Introduce a sentence-long quotation in your own words. (Because the author's name is included in the following sentence, it does not have to be included in the parentheses.) Jones's novel *An Odd Day* opens with the description, **"On the first morning after the visit, the people of Highbury woke up to a yellow sky with a purple sun"** (173).
Parts of one or more sentences	To quote part of a sentence, introduce it with your own words. Use ellipsis points [. . .] to indicate any portion of text you have omitted. Bracket words you have added to help the quotation make sense. Ms. Ainslie surprised everyone by wearing a top hat as she **"jogged down the path at a moderate pace . . . [and] sneered at the people sitting on the benches that lined the path"** (North 267).
Long passage (more than four lines)	Introduce a long quotation with a sentence that ends with a colon. Indent the quotation one-half inch from the left margin. Do not place it in quotation marks. The serious nature of Bartholomew's thoughts is reflected in his following statement: **The problem is that I don't know what to do about this situation. I'm not exactly sure who I can talk to, and I've been lying awake nights trying to figure it out. I wish that some sort of book existed where I could find the answers to all of my problems, but I suppose there are no easy answers.** (French 754)

ACTIVITY
Reread the long passage quoted in the chart, and write the following with proper citation:

1. A sentence quoting a word or phrase from it

2. A one-sentence quotation from that passage with an introduction

3. A passage quoting one or more sentences, using ellipsis points to indicate that material has been omitted

Research and Report Writing

Activity

Documenting Sources Within the Paper

When you are writing your paper, remember that you must document, or cite, sources for paraphrased material as well as for direct quotations. Two common methods of documentation are discussed on this sheet.

The first method of documenting sources is to use documentation notes. To do this, place a number directly after each item to be documented. This number should be slightly above the line (see example below) and after any punctuation marks. Then the actual documentation note should appear with a corresponding number in one of two forms, depending on its placement:

- **Footnote:** This is a documentation note that appears at the bottom of the page.
- **Endnote:** This is a documentation note that appears at the end of the text of the paper on a separate page titled "Notes."

Here are examples of a footnote and endnote that refer to the following sentence in a research paper:

In fact, some scholars have stated that the lack of produce available that year led to an increase in the number of childhood illnesses.[1]

Footnote

amount of childhood illnesses.[1]

[1]John Anson, Drought (New York: Paulsen Press, 1999) 37.

Single-space footnote, Double-space between footnotes

Endnote

Notes

[1]John Anson, Drought (New York:

Paulsen Press, 1999) 37.

Double-space endnote, Double-space between endnotes

The second method of documenting sources is to use parenthetical documentation, a simple notation of the author's name and a page number in parentheses at the end of the sentence. An example follows.

Scholars speculate that the lack of fruits and vegetables available that year led to an increased number of childhood illnesses. (Anson 526).

When you use parenthetical documentation, follow these instructions:

- Do not repeat the author's name in the parenthetical citation if you use it within the sentence or paragraph. For example, *Anson says that illnesses increased* (526).
- Do not separate pieces of information with commas or periods.
- Put the parentheses inside the final punctuation mark of the sentence.

Research and Report Writing
Activity

When you use parenthetical documentation, different kinds of sources require slightly different notations. The chart that follows illustrates the documentation situations you are most likely to encounter.

Citing from . . .	How to Document
A work with one author	Place the author's last name and the page number in parentheses.
A work with two authors	List both authors' last names before the page number.
A work with three or more authors	Use the last name of the first author and the abbreviation *et al.* (meaning "and others") before the page number.
A work with no author or editor	Use the title and the page number.
Material from two or more sources by the same author	Use the author's name, the title of the work, and the page number.
More than one source for the same material	Use the appropriate documentation for all sources.

ACTIVITY A
Shown below are two note cards and a paragraph a student wrote, using the notes on those cards. Look at the note cards and the paragraph. Then decide where in the paragraph the citations should go and cite the correct source. Use parenthetical documentation.

It's Great to Be Me Allen   1
Reaction to reviews

Johnson expressed disbelief to Allen that
they gave good reviews with so many flaws.

3   page 37

L. D. Johnson: An Incredibly Human   2
Hero Zorn
Johnson's plans
"Johnson planned a bizarre remake. He had
this crazy idea of using dogs and cats in the
lead roles."

7   page 175

    Johnson won numerous awards for his movie *Hello*. Despite all the acclaim, Johnson did not like the film. In her autobiography, actress Damaris Allen says that Johnson couldn't believe such a flawed film received such good reviews. Johnson went on to make other award-winning films, but he never stopped thinking about *Hello*. He wanted to remake it. According to a close friend, "He had this crazy idea of using dogs and cats in the lead roles." This desire was never fulfilled, and Johnson died soon after.

ACTIVITY B
Listed below are the sources used for the paragraph above. Rewrite the sources as either footnotes or endnotes.

Allen, Damaris. *It's Great To Be Me.* New York: Gwen Press: 1998.

Zorn, Phillip. *L. D. Johnson: An Incredibly Human Hero.* Los Angeles: George B. Kaht, 1999.

Research and Report Writing
Activity

Compiling a List of Works Cited

The last page (or pages) of your research paper should contain a list of works cited. This list verifies that you used reliable sources in support of your statements, and it allows your readers to locate and consult any of your sources for their own reference.

The chart that follows gives examples of bibliographic entries for the most common types of sources. Use these examples as models when you compile your own list of works cited.

Source	Format for List of Works Cited
Book with one author	Stelley, Diane G. *Beekeeping: An Illustrated Handbook.* Blue Ridge Summit, PA: Tab Books, 1993.
Book with two authors	Markham, Ron, and Cheryl Courson. *The Handbook of Beekeeping.* Ithaca, NY: Cornell University Press, 1996.
Book with three or more authors	Sammataro, et al. *The Beekeeper's Handbook.* Dexter, MI: Peach Mountain Press, 1987.
Article in periodical	Johnson, Sally A. "A Beekeeper's Year." *Apiculture* Sept. 1999: 40–44.
Article in newspaper	Bertram, Jeffrey. "African Bees: Fact or Myth?" *Orlando Sentinel* Aug. 18, 1999: D2.
Encyclopedia article	"Honeybees." *The Oxford Book of Insects.* New York: Oxford University Press, 1989.
Personal interview	Seidler, Harold. Personal interview. May 25, 1999.
Videocassette	*Beekeeping.* Videocassette. University of North Carolina Extension Office, 1999.
Audiocassette	*Easy Beekeeping.* Audiocassette. University of North Carolina Extension Office, 1998.
CD-ROM	Bee Flight. CD-ROM. Baltimore, MD: *Flights of Fancy,* 1999.
Web site	Sanford, Malcolm T. "Small Hive Beetle." *Bee Culture* Feb. 4, 1999. July 17, 1999 http://bee.airoot.com/beeculture/99feb/99feb4.html.

The format for the entries in the list is the same as the format you used on your bibliography cards. If you prepared your bibliography cards carefully, you can simply transfer the information to your list of works cited. Follow these guidelines:

- Alphabetize entries in the list of works cited by author's last name. If no author is given, alphabetize by editor's or compiler's last name. If no author, editor, or compiler is given, alphabetize by the first word in the title of the work. (Disregard the articles *a, an,* and *the* when you are alphabetizing.)
- Sort through your bibliography cards, alphabetizing them. You can then go through the pack, transferring the necessary information to the list one card at a time.
- Begin your list of works cited on a new page at the end of your paper.
- Center the title "Works Cited" at the top of the page.
- Double-space all lines of type on the page. Do not leave any extra space between entries.

Research and Report Writing
Activity

- Start each entry at the left margin. If an entry is more than one line long, indent the second and following lines one-half inch from the left margin. (See the table on page 35, noting how entries are indented.)
- In general, information in bibliographic entries falls in this order: author, title of work, publication information. However, keep in mind that you must make format changes in the following situations: For an entry with multiple authors, reverse only the first and last names of the first author. For an entry with no author, list the editor first; if there is no editor, start with the title.
- When you cite an entry with page numbers, the numbers should reflect the entire length of the work as opposed to the pages from which you took information, that is the specific pages listed in your parenthetical documentation or in your footnotes or endnotes.
- End all citations with a period.

ACTIVITY A

Suppose that you have completed your paper on beekeeping and must now arrange the bibliographic entries from the table on this worksheet in alphabetical order. On a separate sheet of paper, write the first word of each entry in the order in which it should appear on your list of works cited.

ACTIVITY B

Imagine that a student who is researching the influence of Eleanor Roosevelt has not prepared his bibliography cards carefully. He recorded as much publication information as he could find, but he did not do it in a standard format. Using the information on this student's bibliography cards, create a list of works cited, on a separate sheet of paper. You will have to sort out the information on these cards to create properly organized and formatted entries.

This I Remember, book by Eleanor Roosevelt herself. New York, Harper & Row, 1949

Ray Spangenburg and Diane K. Moser, coauthors. Eleanor Roosevelt: A Passion to Improve 1997: Facts on File, New York

Web site: http://ervk.org on April 4th, 1999 ERVK: The Eleanor Roosevelt Center at Val-Kill Updated Mar. 18, 1999. Maintained by the Eleanor Roosevelt Center

Elliott Roosevelt [Eleanor's son] book title: Eleanor Roosevelt, With Love: A Centenary Remembrance, 1994 Published by Dutton in New York

page 22 in Time magazine "Return Visit: Eleanor Roosevelt" November 2, 1942

VCI Home Video The Eleanor Roosevelt Story— VCI Home Video 1996 Video

Research and Report Writing
Activity

Revising a Rough Draft

After you have completed your rough draft and gotten all your ideas down on paper, you are ready to start the revision process. Revising a draft entails carefully examining your paper, making improvements, and correcting any mistakes. Set your draft aside for a day. Then review it carefully.

When you revise a draft, your first concern should be organization. Look for complete thoughts that flow smoothly and logically from one to the next. Concentrate on whether your paper makes sense.

In the left column of the following chart are some questions to ask yourself as you revise your rough draft. In the right column are suggestions for what to do if you answer yes to the questions in the left column.

If Your Answer to This Question Is Yes . . .	You Might Want to Try This:
Do I cover too many subjects?	Review your thesis statement. Is it clear and focused? Make sure the material in your paper supports the thesis. Take out any material that does not.
Does the point of my paper—my argument—get lost somewhere in the middle?	Double-check transitions and the logical flow of information. (Go back to your outline; it may help.) Watch out for unrelated ideas that cloud the main issue. If you find any, take them out or move them.
Do my paragraphs seem choppy?	Find the transition words at the beginnings of your paragraphs. If you cannot find any, add them. If transition words are already there, try using different ones.
Does my introduction seem disconnected from the body of my paper?	Add a transition word, phrase, or sentence at the end of the introduction or the beginning of the body.
Are my sentences boring? Do they all seem to be the same length?	Avoid repeating words, particularly adjectives. Use precise, descriptive words. Revise sentences so they are of varying lengths.
Am I talking down to my audience? Am I talking over my readers' heads?	Make sure that you define special terms or vocabulary. Also make sure that you explain your statements clearly and fully.

Since you want to be certain of the accuracy of your quotations, you should go back and check them against your note cards. If they still sound odd, revisit the source and double-check to make sure that you copied the material as it appears.

If possible, give your draft to someone else to read. You might ask this person to answer the questions from the chart above. Ask your reviewer also to check your organization and logic. After you receive the reviewer's feedback, you can decide which suggestions you intend to follow and make the necessary changes to your paper.

Following is a portion of a student's rough draft. As he went over it, he made corrections and wrote notes in the margins. He will make some of the changes later, after he has reviewed the entire draft.

Research and Report Writing
Activity

> What do
> ~~We've all read or heard about~~ the spotted owl, the bald eagle, and
>   have in common? We've been told that if
> the Siberian tiger. ~~If~~ we don't stop building houses and cutting down
>   our actions
> trees and hunting, ~~it~~ actions could lead to the extinction of these
>
> animals. Conservationists are working hard to make sure this doesn't
>
> happen. These particular species are the "cute and cuddly" ones, the
>
> ones that get attention in the newspapers. People seem to care about
>   these   such as
> what happens to ~~animals~~. What about other species, ~~like~~ toads, fish, and
>   (not a species)   South American frogs
> (wild honeybees)? Does it really matter if a few kinds of ~~somethings~~ disap-
> pear from the earth forever? The answer, according to scientists all over
>   resounding   These scientists want to make biodiversity
> the world, is a ~~loud~~ yes.   a household word.
>
> (move to end of ¶) The impact of humans on the earth's biodiversity is a matter of
>
> increasing concern as species disappear fast. One biologist calls what is
>
> (thesis- ok here?) happening "a worldwide epidemic of extinctions." (card 29) Biodiversity (check quotation)
>
> is the name for the "intricate web of animals, plants, and all other living
>
> things that populate the planet." (card 15) Biodiversity refers to the number
>
> of species as well as to the genetic diversity within species. The importance
>   understood
> of biodiversity is only beginning to be ~~known~~.

ACTIVITY

The two paragraphs below are from the same rough draft of the paper on biodiversity. Use the questions in the chart on this sheet to help you evaluate the draft. Make needed revisions by rewriting the paragraphs on a separate piece of paper.

Let's review the numbers, shall we? A research biologist from the University of Tennessee, Stuart Pimm, calculates that some 50 percent of the world's species could be in danger of extinction in another hundred years. (card 18) That includes mammals, plants, birds, fish, and insects. Pimm believes that 11 percent of bird species, or 1,100 of the nearly 10,000 species, are "on the edge of extinction." (card 20) Even the Cape Sable sparrow is headed for extinction. The picture for plants is no better, according to a respected team of botanists—people who study plants. Their findings: one-eighth of the earth's plants is at risk of becoming extinct. (card 34)

They understand that extinction is happening everywhere. It's not just in the rain forests or in the disappearing wetlands—it's everywhere. The most recent period— the one that killed off the dinosaurs—was caused by a meteorite that crashed into the earth in a blaze of fire. The rate of extinction, report experts, is even greater than what occurred 65 million years ago when the dinosaurs were dying out.

Research and Report Writing
Activity

Editing and Proofreading

After you have revised your draft and feel confident about the content of your paper, you can proceed to the next step, editing and proofreading. You should edit and proofread your paper to eliminate errors in grammar, spelling, and punctuation. After you have put so much effort into your paper, you do not want to submit it with errors that could have been easily corrected.

The greater part of editing and proofreading is paying attention to the smallest details. When you edit and proofread, go through your entire paper a number of times, checking for one type of error at a time. For example, when you focus on spelling, check the spelling of any words you are unsure about, names of people and places, and foreign words. One certain way to make yourself slow down and really see the spelling of each word is to read your paper aloud from back to front. If you are working on computer, do not rely completely on your spelling program because it will not pick up certain types of errors (*sent* used when you mean *scent; won* instead of *one*).

When you check for errors, read slowly and look for the following:

- All sentences are complete.
- There are no missing words.
- Every word says just what you want it to say, and you are absolutely sure of its meaning. Consult a dictionary or a thesaurus if necessary.
- The subjects and verbs agree and verb tenses are consistent.
- All pronouns agree in number and gender with the nouns they stand for, and it is clear what person, people, or objects the pronouns refer to.
- The first word of every sentence is capitalized properly as are proper nouns and acronyms.
- Sentences and documentation facts are punctuated correctly.
- All parentheses and quotation marks appear in pairs.

ACTIVITY
Use the strategies discussed on this page to proofread the following paragraph. Correct all the errors you find.

Many applications of technology during the Civil War should recieve attention. People had flown in lighter-than-air balloons before the war, but Thaddeus Lowe was first to locate enemy positons from the vantage point of his balloon basket. On the communications front. the telegraph had been around for some years. However, the civil war was the first war in which the telegraph played a "crucial role. 12 Prior to the war, railroads was just beginning to boom. Only after the war started did people realise how valuable the railroads were. Railroad tracks and bridges become frequent targets of enemy atack. Crippling the enemies means of transportation was an accepted and usually effective battle strategy.

Research and Report Writing
Activity

Presenting the Paper

For a writer, presentation means how a finished research paper looks to the reader. The reader should take one look and want to continue reading the paper. Remember that format affects the reader even before content has a chance to, so you will want to take some time to ensure that your paper appears professional.

Preparing a paper for presentation involves one last check to make sure you followed formatting instructions, included all necessary information, and created a neat final product. Your teacher may also have given you specific instructions about a cover sheet or other format issues.

The following characteristics describe a research paper that is ready for presentation:

Content
- The title reflects the content and purpose of the paper.
- The introduction engages the audience and gives a clear sense of the purpose of the paper.
- Ideas are organized logically.
- The language level of the paper is appropriate for the audience.
- The text contains no omitted words and no errors in grammar, usage, punctuation, capitalization, or spelling.
- The sources of all quoted and paraphrased material, data, and statistics are credited appropriately.
- Source documentation is accurate and complete.

Format
- All pages are neat and clean.
- All pages are included, in order, and held together with a staple, paper clip, or according to the teacher's instructions.
- Any last-minute corrections of errors are invisible or barely noticeable.
- All pages, starting with page 2, are numbered sequentially, including the page for works cited.
- The required identifying information (student's name, teacher's name, class, and date) appears on separate double-spaced lines on the first page of the paper or on a cover page, as instructed by the teacher.
- There is a one-inch margin at the top, bottom, and both sides of every page.
- All text is double-spaced, including long quotations and entries in the list of works cited.
- Footnotes are single-spaced.

The next time you prepare a research paper for presentation, use the two-part list on this sheet as a checklist.

ACTIVITY
Locate a research paper you previously wrote for a class. Evaluate it according to the presentation checklist on this sheet. Does your paper comply with the qualities described in the list? Write a paragraph explaining what you would have to do, if anything, to bring your paper in line with the items on the checklist.

Answers

Choosing a Topic for Research
Students' responses will vary but may include the following: Harriet Tubman was the inspired "conductor" on the Underground Railroad.

Setting a Schedule
Students' schedules will vary but should contain the steps of prewriting, research, drafting, and revising for two papers. The schedules must be broken down into appropriate time frames so that both reports are completed in four weeks; more time will probably be allocated to the history paper since it must be twice the length of the science paper.

Finding Information and Evaluating It
1. Unreliable; this veterinarian may be trying to promote a product.
2. Not certain; you must do more research before you can determine whether information on a personal Web site is reliable.
3. Reliable; the business owner has had a great deal of experience in the field.

Conducting Personal Interviews
Students' oral reports should indicate that they followed the ten steps to obtain effective information, and their analysis should indicate that they can evaluate their own strengths and weaknesses.

Conducting Library Research
Students' lists will vary but must contain one of each of the following types of resources: a book; a dictionary, encyclopedia, atlas, or almanac; an index; a periodical; an audiocassette, videotape, or CD-ROM; a computer resource; a resource from a special collection.

Using the *Readers' Guide to Periodical Literature*
1. BALTIMORE ORIOLES (BASEBALL TEAM)
2. yes; because il means illustrated
3. B. Olney
4. October 18, 1998
5. pages 94–95

Using Computer Catalogs and Indexes in the Library
Students' responses will vary but may resemble the following: An author search was done for Twain, Mark. One hundred and fifty-four entries matched. One entry was for the title *Mark Twain's Fables of Man,* published in Berkeley by the University of California Press in 1992. The call number is 818 CLE.

Searching on the Internet
1. Students' answers will vary but may include this key-word search: Thomas AND Jefferson AND religious freedom.
2. As sites are added or deleted, the number of matches will vary, but students could find up to nine thousand or more sites.
3. Answers will vary, but students may find three sites with relevant information.
4. Students may say yes, they would change religious freedom to Virginia Statute of Religious Freedom in the key-word search.

Evaluating Internet Sources
Students' responses will vary but should have the kind of information contained in this example: childhood AND immunization AND effectiveness; the Web site is KidsHealth; the address is http://kidshealth.org/parent/healthy/vaccine/ html; the publisher is the Nemours Foundation. Responses to the evaluation questions will differ but should indicate that the student has critically evaluated the accuracy of the information presented on the site and assigned a score that is logical on the basis of the evaluation.

Using CD-ROMs
Activity A
Students' responses will vary according to the source used, but they may include the following: *The World Book Multimedia Encyclopedia* CD-ROM's entry for the solar system has no graphics but says that the solar system is part of the Milky Way Galaxy. There is a related articles topic for the Milky Way. The article for the Milky Way shows a picture of the Milky Way Galaxy and explains where Earth is located. The text and photos help give an understanding of Earth's place in the solar system and the Milky Way.

Activity B
Students' responses should demonstrate the use of problem-solving skills to plan a trip with the help of a special-topic CD-ROM, given a starting point, a destination, and a side trip.

Using Other Electronic Sources
Activity A
Students' responses will vary, according to their choices, but may resemble the following: Audiocassette: Title, *The Taming of the Shrew* Sound Recording; Producer, none listed; call number, 822.33 SHA CASS

Answers

Activity B

Students' responses will vary but may include the following:

5. A videocassette about *A Tale of Two Cities* might show a movie version of the story, which would provide visual details about characters and setting.

6. DVD on firefighting techniques might provide film footage showing the different techniques used in fighting different types of fires. It might also contain accounts of historical fires and sound recordings of eyewitness accounts of fires (such as an actor reading from Samuel Pepys's diary entry on the Great Fire of London in 1666).

7. An audiocassette of 1960s songs would convey a flavor of the times and offer insight into the state of recording equipment and technology.

Preparing Note Cards

Students' responses should demonstrate the ability to create note cards following a specified format. Here is an example of a paraphrased statement:

> Clark was originally hesitant, but she overcame this and led a brilliant political life. Her speeches focused on reforming and creating a more compassionate society. Her audience, including many women who were exercising their voting rights for the first time, agreed with her. She was elected senator.

Here is an example of a summary statement:

Clark had a brilliant political career once she erased her self-doubts. Her passionate speeches convinced voters, many of whom were women voting for the first time, to elect her to the Senate.

Avoiding Plagiarism

Students' responses will vary, but here is an example of a paragraph that is properly cited:

> For good reading skills to develop, it is important that parents set a time to read with their children every night (Nelson 78). According to L. T. Nelson, the time parents spend reading with their children is "magical" (92). This is a good way to encourage children to read. However, since children may want to read on their own, it is important that parents keep books around the house that children find interesting (109).

Developing a Working Bibliography

(Note that indents for notes or bibliographical data are not shown in these answers.)

Students' answers should indicate that the following books are appropriate for a report on Lan:

1. Rone, Ida. *60s Folk Artists.* Chicago: AB Press, 1998. This book probably includes information on Lan even though it may also discuss Doe.

2. Trent, B. *Sarita's Rise.* Miami: Nod, 1998.

3. Ar, Cyrus. *Doe, Lan, Smid, and Teag: Four Legends.* Memphis: Moose Press, 1997. Both of these books contain information on Lan.

Creating Bibliography Cards for Books

1. Source 1 Schmitz, David F. *Architects of the American Century.* Chicago: Imprint Publications, 1999. Morris County Public Library Call No. 765.82 Sch

2. Source 2 Heath, David. Congress of the United States. Mankato, MN: Capstone Press, 1999. Morris High School Call No. 760.32 Hea

Creating Bibliography Cards for Periodicals

1. Russo, R. M., and Paul G. Silver. "The Andes' Deep Origins." Natural History Feb. 1995: 52–92.

2. Moffat, Anne Simon. "Biogeographers Take a New View of the Ancient Andes." Science June 7, 1996: 1420–21.

Creating Bibliography Cards for Videocassettes, Films, and Audiocassettes

Kingdom of the Sun: Peru's Inca Heritage. Perf. David Lewiston. Audiocassette. Elektra/Nonesuch, 1998.

Creating Bibliography Cards for CD-ROMs

Activity A

3D Atlas. CD-ROM. Vers. 2.1. Batlas Arts, 1997.

Activity B

Students' cards will vary but may include entries organized and punctuated like this: Explorers of the New World. CD-ROM. Cambridge, MA: SoftKey Multimedia, 1996.

Creating Bibliography Cards for Other Electronic Sources

1. Eyewitness Children's Encyclopedia. Diskette. DK Multimedia, 1998.

2. Mountain Music of Peru. Smithsonian/Folkways, Prod. Rounder Records, 1994.

Answers

Creating Bibliography Cards for On-line Sources

Dillon, Michael, and Nancy Hensold. "Environments." Andean Botanical Information System. Mar. 2, 1999. The Field Museum, Chicago, IL. Mar. 3, 1999 http://www.sacha.org

Organizing Note Cards

Activity A

Students' responses should indicate that the best approach for this topic is chronological.

Activity B

Students' responses will differ; they should demonstrate the ability to recognize that either the cause-and-effect approach or the chronological approach is appropriate for this topic. The cards should be divided into a cause section and an effect section or into a before section and an after section. Subtopics might include the price of personal computers, the type of information accessible on personal computers, and the rise of electronic mail.

Developing an Outline

Students' outlines will vary but may approximate the following:

I. Classroom training
   A. Number of hours required
   B. Sources of classroom training
II. Behind-the-wheel training
   A. Number of hours required
   B. Sources of behind-the-wheel training
III. Preparing for and taking the drivers' test
   A. How to study and prepare
   B. Where and when to take the test

Developing a Thesis Statement

Students' responses should identify item 2 as the best thesis statement.

Item 1 reports what one firm recommends.

Item 3 states an opinion but is too general to serve as the basis of a research report.

Writing a Research Paper That Explains a Process

The items numbers should be in the following order: 5, 7, 1, 11, 4, 6, 2, 10, 9, 8, 3.

Writing a Research Paper That Compares and Contrasts

Activity A

Students' diagrams should indicate that both countries are coastal and popular with tourists but that A is rich, industrial, and has rain forests, whereas B is poor, agricultural, and has deserts.

Activity B

Students' outlines will vary but should follow either the block method or feature-by-feature method shown on the worksheet. Features the students should focus on include the location, land features, industries, and economies of the two countries.

Writing a Research Paper That Explains Cause and Effect

Activity A

Students' responses should indicate that the most effective way to discuss campaign tactics is probably to focus on the causes of the candidate's successful campaign. Focusing on sequence of events would be unsuitable because the candidate probably used several strategies or tactics at once.

Activity B

Students' sequence chains will vary but must demonstrate the students' ability to recognize cause-and-effect relationships within a topic of their own choosing and to create a sequence chain reflecting those relationships.

Revising an Outline

Students' responses will vary but may resemble the following:

I. In the past
   A. Written correspondence
      1. Invitations
         a. official
         b. informal
      2. Thank-you letters
      3. Business correspondence
      4. Friendly letters
   B. Telephone communication
      1. Busy signals
      2. No answer
      3. Direct conversation, not messages
   C. Telegraph communication
      1. Fast overseas communication
      2. Ship-to-shore communication

Answers

Formatting a Research Paper

Students' typed page should show that they allowed a one-inch margin around the page, double-spaced all text, listed their identifying information in the upper right corner, centered the title, and indented the first line of the opening paragraph.

Writing a Rough Draft

Students' responses should be as follows:

1. Don't necessarily write the introduction first. Ideas for this may come to you as you write the body of your rough draft.
2. Don't waste time now thinking about exact wording. Put down the best word you can think of, circle it, and go on.
3. Write transitions as you go, but plan on checking them later.

Using Quotations

Students' responses will vary, but they may be formatted and punctuated as shown in the following examples:

1. When he says, "I don't know what to do about this situation," Bartholomew indicates his confusion. (French 754)
2. French underscores how deeply Bartholomew is disturbed when he quotes Bartholomew as saying, "I'm not exactly sure who I can talk to and I've been lying awake nights trying to figure it out" (French 754).
3. Bartholomew confides that his situation is really disturbing him, saying, "I'm not exactly sure who I can talk to. . . . [and] I wish that some sort of book existed where I could find the answers to all of my problems." (French 754).

Documenting Sources Within the Paper

Activity A

Students' responses should be
    reviews (37).
    roles" (Zorn 175).

Activity B

Students' responses should be
    reviews.[1]
    roles."[2]

    [1]Damaris Allen, *It's Great to Be Me* (New York: Gwen Press, 1998) 37.

    [2]Phillip Zorn, *L. D. Johnson: An Incredibly Human Hero* (Los Angeles: George B. Kaht, 1999) 175.

Compiling a List of Works Cited

Activity A

1. Bee	7. Markham
2. Beekeeping	8. Sammataro
3. Bertram	9. Sanford
4. Easy	10. Seidler
5. "Honeybees"	11. Stelley
6. Johnson	

Activity B

The Eleanor Roosevelt Center. ERVK: The Eleanor Roosevelt Center at Val-Kill. Mar. 18, 1999. Apr. 4, 1999 http://ervk.org.

The Eleanor Roosevelt Story. Videocassette. VCI Home Video, 1996.

"Return Visit: Eleanor Roosevelt." Time Nov. 2, 1942: 22.

Roosevelt, Eleanor. This I Remember. New York: Harper & Row, 1949.

Roosevelt, Elliott. Eleanor Roosevelt, With Love: A Centenary Remembrance. New York: Dutton, 1994.

Spangenburg, Ray, and Diane K. Moser. Eleanor Roosevelt: A Passion to Improve. New York: Facts on File, 1997.

Revising a Rough Draft

Students' paragraphs may contain revisions similar to the following:

1. Review the numbers for yourself.
2. Included in Pimm's account are mammals
3. Here is a specific example: Pimm believes that 11 percent
4. Their findings indicate that
5. The scientists understand that extinction is happening all over the world.

Editing and Proofreading

Students' responses should contain the following corrections:

    receive attention; was the first; enemy positions; front, the; the Civil War; "crucial role" (Author, 12).; railroads were just; people realize; bridges became; enemy attack; enemy's means

Presenting the Paper

Students' responses will vary but should demonstrate the ability to evaluate a paper according to a given set of guidelines involving the content and format of a research paper in its final form.